Black Box Poetics
Short Memoirs of Chaos

Kendall Johnson

BAMBOO
DART
PRESS

LOS ANGELES † NEW YORK † LONDON † MELBOURNE

Black Box Poetics by Kendall Johnson

ISBN: 978-1-947240-22-3

eISBN: 978-1-947240-23-0

First Printing 2021

For information:

Bamboo Dart Press

chapbooks@bamboodartpress.com

Curated and operated by Dennis Callaci and Mark Givens

Bamboo Dart Press 009

Pelekinesis
www.pelekinesis.com

BAMBOO DART PRESS
www.bamboodartpress.com

SHRiMPER
www.shrimperrecords.com

TABLE OF CONTENTS

Introduction: I have a closet, tucked away...

Black Box Poetics is dedicated with great joy and love
to my wife Susan Ilsley.

PROLOGUE

I Have a Closet, Tucked Away

A set of thirty rectangular black wooden boxes, perhaps twelve inches long and ten inches wide, and an inch deep, with a two small handles on each side line the shelves of one of my closets. The boxes are identical but are neither named nor numbered. Each has a clasp holding the lid shut, though I suspect for different reasons. Each of the lids on top is clear glass with a quarter inch frame, again, black. Each of the black boxes contains white pages, typed, one or two pages each, stapled at the top left corner. 300-500 word stories. The stories are quite true, unfortunately.

These are the stories I said I'd never write. The kind of stories, once heard, you can't erase from your mind. Scenes you wish you'd never seen. Sensations you wish never to feel again. When I began writing, photography, and painting, I adopted what is rightly or wrongly termed the Hippocratic Oath that medical people are bound by: simply, do no harm. I've held these stories back.

Stories can hurt, they can expose others to images and realities that, like the proverbial earwigs, can work their way into the brain and cause chaos. The point of my work as a therapist and crisis counselor, as well as an artist, is to protect my readers and viewers from pain, not to cause it. I've softened this view somewhat. Lately I've come to think that sometimes it's helpful to know that there are, scary and troublesome or not, some things that do go bump in the night.

All of the stories in the boxes, all bound tight and stuck away, are either my own direct experience or the direct experience relayed to me by the person involved that I know to have been there. I have either gotten that person's permission to share their story, or have changed names, gender, location, and/or circumstances to protect that person's privacy. Similarly, I've changed the name and sometimes the type of organizations or agencies, their locations and/or circumstances. Don't bother trying to figure them out; I'm fairly good at deceit.

Flash Burns

Flying

Earth unexpectedly falls away. I fly. Puzzled. Now abruptly I land with a jolt in a pile of arms, legs, equipment and dust, on top of the guy I'd just pulled off a cliff. Scrambling up to see what had happened. Watching the tail end of a huge rattlesnake complete its crossing of the narrow game trail we had been following. I stare at the full two inches of rattles. I must have been about to step on it.

Each time I tell the story I become lost in the fragmentary sensations. It comes alive again, and I see the setting sun making the snake's scales glow amber all over, again. And again. I tell this to my crisis team trainees to illustrate the way the mid-brain triggers muscle reaction before it passes the information through the conscious channels of the upper brain. The brain has learned this lesson through thousands of years of survival. Sometimes you live longer by not taking time to think.

And each time I tell the story to a new class, I smell the tall brush on that narrow game trail. I see how the sky moves from luminous blue, through green, through gold to the setting sun. How we had heard the cries of the man on the cliff across the canyon, had forded the stream, busted brush, found the game trail across the plateau to reach him. How he'd looked confused and betrayed after I—his savior—had landed on him and we'd collapsed in a dusty pile of arms and legs.

Grandma and the Bug

Dorthea had just turned eighty. She lived alone on the end of a street that zagged up a hillside not far from the center of town. On Saturdays she entertained her twenty-two year old grandson, her youngest. He'd come over and work on his Volkswagen Bug in her driveway, and she'd bake him cookies. It was a good deal for both of them.

The street had high curbs, and he'd run the car parallel to the curb with two wheels up. With the clearance afforded by the cheap VW jack, he'd have enough room to work underneath the engine compartment in the back.

And so on this particular Saturday he was underneath and she was inside baking when she thought she heard something funny, so she stuck her head out the door to check. At first things looked all right, then she realized his legs were kicking. As she drew closer, she saw that the jack had collapsed and the car had settled on her grandson. He couldn't breath.

She had no time to make a 9-11 call. 113 pound Dorthea walked over, grabbed the rear bumper, and lifted the rear end of the Volkswagen off her grandson and set it aside. In so doing she ruptured two discs, sprained her right shoulder, tore several muscles, and nearly passed out. And saved her grandson's life.

Later, in the emergency room, her attending physician pointed out some of the wonders of the human body. She'd been flooded by catecholamines that had fueled her body, and also by endogenous opioids that had dulled the pain at the time, dissociated her awareness of emotions so she could function, and gave her the sense of being able to manage. She didn't panic and just did what she needed to do.

The fear and pain all came later.

Flashback

As the series of fires broke out, coordination of resources and manpower were necessary, and a unified command set up. A mental health resource with fire experience, I was passed up the evolving commands until I ended up being the stress consultant to all of the fourteen major conflagrations burning from Simi Valley to the Mexican border. The "Fire Siege of 2003" had already killed five. Four days into it, my job was to deploy my people, to conduct debriefings, advise commanders on stress management, and to help the teams stay focused.

I sat in on a meeting while a fire crew recounted a burn-over where they just about lost everything. The leader of the meeting—an old acquaintance I'd teamed up with before—glanced in my direction and looked concerned.

Suddenly I can't breathe. I know I am sitting safe in this meeting room miles from the fire line, yet I am hit by the all-too-familiar panic of oxygen deprivation and I can't breathe deep enough. The acrid smoke smells of Eucalyptus and sage, and the room has turned dark. My skin is hot through the army blanket I've wrapped over my face, and people near me are yelling. Small points of bright orange light are breaking through the blanket as it begins to burn away. The fire engine drives up the truck trail, right through the fire line. The engine lurches suddenly and my shoulder slams against metal as I try to hold on. The tiny lights grow, and turn into nickel and quarter sized holes. The heat is unbearable and I feel my eyelashes singe. I fight for air.

I regained control, sat through the rest of the meeting, but after it was over, we took a walk. A long one. I had done the same with him on more than one occasion. He had learned his compassion the hard way. We walked along the dirt road for an hour, in the middle of the night. The Santa Ana winds still blowing hot and dry.

He helped me tell the story of my own burn-over thirty years earlier. This time in words, this time more completely, so I could start to let it go and begin to breathe again.

In the Shadow of Twin Towers

09:01 EST

"Dr. Johnson, this is Dr. Emily Cooper of the Chancellor's Office, NYC Schools. You trained our school crisis teams several years ago. Yes. Well, not good right now. I'm looking out my window. I can't see the World Trade Center for the smoke, and it evidently collapsed. The Chancellor has asked that you provide us direction. We don't really know what to do next . . . *(at this point the line goes dead)*."

Within 20 minutes after the first airliner was flown into tower #1, the Chancellor's Office contacted me in California by telephone about 6:00 a.m. my time, describing the situation and requesting consulting assistance. We agreed I would send materials building upon my 1992 trainings provided city-wide, and would personally contact District #3, located at the center of the disaster. At that point, in the middle of the call, the tower collapsed, taking with it the Chancellor's office telephone switchboard that was located in the second tower. We were disconnected. It took days for contact to be resumed. During this time District #3 called (their office was located in Brooklyn, and telephone contact with the District—though not the Chancellor's Office—was quickly re-established) and the District requested additional assistance in person for their crisis team. As the days wore on, materials were sent and plans drawn for the first visit.

When our plane, one of the first to resume flights, landed safely at JFK, the passengers first cheered. Then they got very quiet again.

In the Dark, North Woods

"I am the bread of life; whoever comes to me shall never go hungry, and whoever believes in me will never be thirsty." John 6:35*

Hmmm. A touch more oregano. Ah!

He bent to his work. The kitchen was warm and fragrant, the thin cuts of meat sautéing nicely in the large skillet, and the sauce beginning to bubble. Albinoni's Adagio in G Minor played just loud enough to be heard over the occasional muted noises of pans and spoons. His stew would sit overnight so the flavors could blend. *Perfect.*

William loved to dress to cook, his long-sleeved chef's apron protecting his white sleeves as well as slacks and tie from splatter. When you lived with your mother, it helps to take advantage of her occasional absences to make things special. *Not even she would understand, really.*

He wondered if he had serving dishes large enough. He might have to break out more before tomorrow. *Why was her house adjacent to the field those kids crossed on their way to school?*

Give us today, our daily bread. Matthew 6:11*

The church was different, fair game. They claimed interest in what you truly loved, but their high and holy attitudes placed limits on their acceptance. So hypocritical! Oh well, their loss. The community had been rocked by the disappearance of several of their children and some in adjacent towns since his arrival in town, and they sought comfort in each other's company.

Comfort he could provide as he shared their loss. His inviting their young parent group over for fellowship tomorrow, lunch being his treat, was perfect. He could cook for larger groups, it was the least he could do. They want communion? He'd give them a communion they would never forget.

Share in my body, share in my blood. He grinned in anticipation, pleased he'd remembered to draw off some liquid. *Crackers and wine just don't cut it.* The idea of those pious Christers swallowing their children . . . he shuddered with pleasure.

He checked his hand-written recipe one more time and smiled. *Little boy stew.*

Whoever eats my flesh and drinks my blood

abides in me, and I in him." John 6:56*

Oh God yes, more salt.

* New International Version

Erasure

Eating the Darkness

"Holy snakes! Really?" Dr. Williams stopped in his tracks. I went to see him as my therapist when things got rough in my consulting work, and I needed him now. "You really worked with a cannibal? Ate people?"

I looked at him. "Children, in fact. And it was sexual. He was a serial killer who raped, tortured and then ate his child victims. On parole from a series of molestation busts on the east coast, but they never figured him for a rapist/killer as well. I did mostly distance consultation with the police."

"To catch the guy?"

"No, he'd already been caught. But the searches of his place started to turn up evidence. Bones, for instance, under his house. And recipes. They contacted me to help them plan how to work with the church and school. He fed parts of one of his victims to his church group, and they wanted to figure how to inform those involved all at once, and in as non-damaging way as possible."

"That they had . . . eaten a child?" Dr. Williams looked pale. "A dark communion! Damn." He was a priest turned therapist.

"That was part of the problem; the other part was that they didn't want CNN to blow the whistle before they could contact all of the folks involved. Time crunch. Imagine finding out you'd been deceived like that. In church."

"Ok. Let's think about this. You wouldn't be here if it wasn't hard. What about this thing is the hardest for you personally?"

I closed my eyes and let images come and go. It was like watching a dust storm, only poorly lit with indistinct forms moving about. I finally settled on a couple things. First, just the idea that someone, somebody's next door neighbor, could actually do that. Fantasy is one thing; the depravity, the inner . . ."

"What was the other?" Dr. Williams asked gently.

"The total perversion of all that is good, I guess." I shook my head slowly, feeling the nausea. "I've got problems with religion, its hypocrisy and coercion, but this . . . to deliberately turn people's best intentions into a horrible outcome in which they themselves were a part." I paused. "That son of a bitch. He fed children to a church group." I shuddered.

Williams nodded slowly.

Your Tax Dollars at Work

They drop you somewhere north of the DMZ, usually alone. You go to create maximum terror—within time and equipment restraints—to undermine local village support for the enemy government who cannot protect them. Sometimes assassination, often you target entire small villages.

You move in darkness. Much of the killing you do silently, by knife. Sometimes by hand. You'd save a few of the girls and boys, a few women, and two or three village elders, all tied. The rest you leave dead.

The elders you tie to stakes in the center of the village, in front of a fire for light. Their bodies and heads you tape in place and cut their eye lids off so they must watch, and you feed them LSD to enhance their experience. The villagers you parade before them, one or two at a time. Some you kill, some you force to kill their children or parents, and some you force to rape. Heads are left on stakes in the firelight. By the time the atrocities are done, all were dead except those elders.

By then it is close to morning. You exfiltrate quietly, usually by helicopter from an adjacent ridge. You leave the elders alive so that they will run to other villages nearby, to bear witness to the demons who will come for them in the night.

Parts Salvage

The little girl had been sucked into a drain pipe that channeled the creek under the road and out the other side. The last of the spring run off was too strong for her to escape and had pinned her against an iron rebar gate, designed to prevent branches and large rocks from blocking it up. She'd been stuck, her lungs had filled with water, and she'd drowned. They might not even have spotted her down in the water, were it not for the flash of her new yellow dress.

I sat with the crew the next day, trying to sort out what had happened and how it was affecting them. Trying to find something to say. We went around the group, replaying what each had seen and felt. Each assured the other that they'd done all they could. When we'd rehashed the circumstances, searched for anything else they could have done to change the outcome, made safety recommendations for others, it didn't feel finished.

They still were avoiding eye contact, and glanced back and forth at each other. They wanted more but looked ready to bolt. The death of a child is always distressing, but the entire crew seemed disproportionately disturbed. They were an emergency crew and dealt with injured and even dead children now and then. I sensed there remained things unsaid. While that is always their choice it seemed from their breathing and tenseness they actually wanted me to coax it forth. I pressed further. "What else?" I ventured.

"We couldn't get the body out," one, older and more experienced firefighter began. "The current kept the body stuck and you just can't turn off a river, it's power." The others nodded, waiting.

"We had to dissemble the body," the Captain finished. "We had to cut it up to get it out."

We were quiet for a minute or so. The older one looked at two of the younger firefighters whose faces streaked with tears. "You know, we get trained for fighting fire, providing first aid, and a little law enforcement. But we're way out in the boonies here, away from medical specialists, and all. Sometimes it's just us. And nothing can train you for this. Nothing."

Loss of Control

Clean cups, move down. It's time to bail.

I just don't want anything to go wrong this time. I'll head up Highway 18 out of Mentone. Once I get up past Forest Falls there are plenty of places where a straight stretch leads to a take off point with at least a couple hundred feet of free fall before impact. In case I fuck it up, I'll fill those two 5-gallon jerry cans of gas and put them in the back seat. Once the car hits, the impact will break the seals on the cans and the thing will would blow up like all of those car chase movies on late night TV. I'll fly like an eagle, like the song says, and let my spirit be free. But shit, what if I lose my nerve at the last minute? Just in case I'll bring along that bottle of Jack Daniels. Must be half of it left. To wash down the pain killers. Back up systems. I got this.

The fire crew that put him out met the next day with the shrink. They'd been dispatched to a car over the side, and pulled hose as a precaution in case there were sparks in the brush, or it caught fire. As they got to the overturned car, it suddenly blew the windows out along with a body, which they hosed down to find was still alive with burns over half of it. Turned out to be male, they discovered when they got the stretcher up to the ambulance and could fish out the guy's wallet and look at his I.D. Highway Patrol opined from the skid marks that he'd lost control and blown his take off.

Laments

Losing Marcie

"Yo, Marco, how are ya, man?"

As a psych disaster consultant, I was on the phone to Marco Benjamin, who ran a disaster team for the Army. Marco is former Long Range Reconnaissance Patrol sergeant with two tours in Nam behind him. Hard guys. Said to jump out of helicopters, terrorize villagers, eat snakes, bugs and the occasional baby. Now out, he runs a unit of disaster workers at a government facility in Maryland. I'd consult with his classes on mental resilience, and after class we'd hang out, drink, and tell war stories.

"What's new this time, Marco, any changes in assignments or procedures?" His trainees were mostly computer people cross-trained to go into the field and help with recovery. A very different kind of stress.

"Well, that's the first thing. When I pick you up at the airport my name will be 'Marcie'."

The tumblers began to click into place. "What?" I started, suspecting that another kind of shoe about to drop.

"Yea. Just brace yourself, you might not recognize me. I'll be dressed in . . you know . . . women's stuff."

We stumbled on a bit longer, and I hung up. *Aw, man.*

Losing Marcie II

Marcie met me at the nearby airport when I arrived—as usual, but different. She looked like a guy in drag, her close-shaved beard lurking under make up. We stood there staring, neither of us knowing quite what to say.

After training, the evening went off as usual, too, sort of. We talked obliquely about the changes. The stress, injections, maybe surgery next year. War stories, now about a different battlefield, a different kind of war. How do you share about "how things were," when everything is in transition? When the what's, and who's and even the is's, are just so many black boxes, and all remaining to be determined?

For months after Marcie began her coming out, we talked back and forth by phone. Marcie was walking a rough road through the unknown, from hard-assed jungle guerrilla fighter to a well over-middle aged woman whose life had upended. She raced through androgynous bars with uncertain intent—first the affair with the gay guy, then the lesbian, then both at once, then neither.

Losing Marcie lll

I wish I could have been a better friend, during her struggles with pronouns, rest rooms, and uncertainty. The Army had been no help preparing her for this battlefield, and she finally lost her job over a lawsuit and a fist fight at work.

Not hearing anything for over a year, I traced Marcie to an apartment near Market Street. An older queen, obviously tired of the struggle, answered the phone when I got through. "Marcie?" she said, sounding like she'd eaten Janice Joplin and broken glass. "I don't know any Marcie, but I do remember a Marco. He's up in the Tenderloin, living off the street."

And that's where I'll find Marcie. She's strong and will be OK. Two tours—in man's land eating snakes. She'll have gotten a new place, better hair-cut and cut of friends, and will seem pleased to see me. She'll be working a queer bar as bouncer. She'll smile.

A Good-bye

As a trauma shrink I had been called in to see Peter Kranz, a 16-year-old boy living with foster parents because of instability in his home. His mother had previously died and his father had begun drinking. His father then died during one of Peter's visits. The courts wanted to ascertain whether he was mentally stable.

His foster mom showed me his room, told me how Peter did his chores, finished homework before TV, decent grades. She was worried, though. "I'm just afraid, Doctor, it's been six months and he hasn't shown any sadness, any anger. I'm afraid he's really depressed. You know, clinically."

I talked with Peter, in his room. He seemed a nice enough kid, smiled and shared some of his interests in music, clothes. He showed me his computer, and a picture of his dad. We talked about the future and where he was in school. I brought the conversation back to his father, wondering if it would elicit a reaction.

"Yeah," he began, "it was really awful. He was having a tough time after my mom had died. Some drinking and not being able to cook and stuff. He'd be gone overnight sometimes. Couldn't share it with me. I'd have to be mother and father. I do that. It hurt my heart to see him like that, so I kept it together. Like I do around here."

"So he was back after one of his several-day benders when he died?" I asked, nudging him to talk about it.

"We were out in the garage. He was crying and apologizing for being gone so much. Told me he loved me. Then all of a sudden he grabbed his arm and fell over. I remembered my CPR and gave him chest compressions like they taught me in P.E. class. And mouth to mouth. The neighbor saw us and called 911 and they finally came. It didn't work, though."

"So he died in your arms? I'm really sorry you had to go through that."

"Yeah," he said, then smiled. "But you know what? I got to kiss him good-bye."

Case Report: Parkinson's Disease

Male, veteran of WWII, diagnosed at 69 years of age with Parkinson's Disease, a progressive neurological debilitation. The patient died seven years later at age 76, being bedridden during the last three years. His struggle with Parkinson's was complicated by severe arthritis, hypoglycemia, and the long-term results of alcoholism. During the last years of his life his tremors were severe, and would exacerbate the arthritic pain such that by 10:00 a.m. most mornings medication could not control the pain without compromising his consciousness. A philosophy professor by trade and a cultured and nuanced man, the patient maintained full cognitive and sensory awareness of his circumstances up until his last month or two, choosing not to be fully sedated because he did not want to miss whatever life he had left. Surprised at having survived the Battle of the Bulge in 1945, the man was not interested in surrendering any more of his remaining life than necessary. He and his wife lived the last several years together in a graduated care facility. She would spend every evening with him.

Following her death ten years later, her personal journal was discovered in her writing desk. One entry was written two months before her husband's death and at the conclusion of their evening visit. At this point he was in extreme pain and could barely articulate well enough for anyone to understand except her. Her entry read:

He leaned up to me and finally was able to say:
"Thank you. It has been worth it. All of it."

Grit

Baghdad

I met Major Sherry Hoyt, USAF (Ret), on the run-up to the attack on Baghdad in 1991. Sherry had served a career as a flight nurse on Medevac flights, and now was heading up an employee assistance program serving George AFB near Adelanto, California. George boasted a Wild Weasel squadron tasked with being the initial assault wave into Baghdad in the coming fight. Sherry knew the reality of combat and knew what was coming.

She asked me to help prepare the George AFB School Crisis Team. The squadron was shipping out in the next two weeks, and the attack would be within the week or so after that. She knew the casualty rate of the crews in the squadron was estimated to be nearly 60%. That meant that over half of the children attending the school were likely to lose one of their parents within hours after the shooting started.

Sherry also knew that of those returning, a high number would be suffering from PTSD. She told me about her own post-Vietnam, post-trauma symptoms.

She said: *I was having flashbacks and nightmares - of body bags, IV's running dry, mounds of blood-soaked bandages. I was filled with feelings of guilt, shame, helplessness, hopelessness and despair. I couldn't sleep, I couldn't concentrate; I, the efficient, organized, competent nurse was falling apart. I felt worthless - I was now a casualty.*

This was why she'd called me, and why on that cold morning in

January, 1991, I was on my way to George AFB. The politicians and generals wanted to save face by spending lives, and a tidal wave of body bags and walking wounded was to be let loose upon an unsuspecting shoreline here at home. Sherry and I might not be able to prevent this fool's-errand attack and the inevitable costs in body and spirit—but we could at least do this. We could train those who would support them, to better serve the survivors and their wounded families.

On Wall Street

Phyllis Bronson had dreamed of a day like today. A school psychologist, she had grown tired of the incessant testing, report writing, and meetings. That's why she'd joined the school crisis team. Yet it wasn't enough, it didn't scratch the itch. She'd used the skills, all right, they were always needed in suicide interventions, parent deaths, conflicts, and all of the normal ills that beset schools.

But Phyll, as she liked to be called, longed for the big one. The air crash, riot, the community disaster. In her team training, the class had culminated with a large incident simulation where all of the micro-skills and tactics had to be orchestrated strategically, complete with complications and time press. She'd been in heaven and ever since had dreamed of an incident of that magnitude.

On the morning of 9/11 it suddenly looked like her wish had come true. Phyll had stopped early at the District Office to pick up some reports, when word came down that a passenger plane had flown into the first tower in the World Trade Center. She stopped in to the office of the director of student services, who was the head of the crisis team, and was told to help call the other team members. While all of the team planning had the members working in groups of three to six, only twenty members had made it to their schools before traffic became gridlocked. One could be spared for each of the closest schools.

She relayed instructions from her team leader to the others:

stay with your school, work in teams of one, do what you can with whatever situation you find. Her school, a specialty high school in the finance district stood within a block of the Trade Center. She drove in as close as she could get, then left her car and walked across Wall Street into the smoke and concrete dust.

Out of There

Back in 1960, wildland fire engines were simpler. No advanced fuel injection. No special air filtration. No on-board computer systems to regulate it all. The pistons were driven by gasoline sprayed into cylinders by carburetors and lit by spark plugs. Usually.

When the unexpected wind blew the fire into reverse and it cornered USFS Engine 2-4 deep in a hollow on their way somewhere else, in this moment of maximum vulnerability and minimal possibility of escape, the motor in 2-4 died. It appeared the crew were all about to fry.

Maybe the air filter clogged, maybe the motor flooded, or perhaps a gas line burst. In any case, the driver couldn't get the motor re-lit, the fire was quickly surrounding them, and the fire engine couldn't get up the truck trail to safety. They were stuck.

Engine Captain Barry Stratford had an idea. While the engineer opened the hood and poked around, Stratford dug around for a coffee can and some tubing. He ordered a crewman to syphon gas out of the tank, enough to fill the coffee can nearly full. Then Stratford ordered another crewman to "swamp us," meaning to call directions to the driver who couldn't see past the raised hood.

Stratford climbed up and perched in the engine compartment, pulled off the air filter, yelled at the driver to start it up, and carefully trickled a small amount of gasoline into the open carburetor. The tall brush on either side of the road were igniting and smoke was blocking vision. The engine fired up.

"Let's get out of here," he ordered, and remained balanced over the motor. He carefully regulated the flow as the truck lurched forward blindly and the driver followed the directions shouted by the crewman who was standing on the running board, keeping them from driving off the road and falling down the mountain and into the fire.

She's Dropping Out

I get to the Nanny Training College dorm by ten that night. The call from the Director had been brief, "You've got to hurry. She's out on the balcony ready to jump. 9-1-1 says their ETA is fifteen minutes. See if you can help." I live five minutes away.

The other girls meet me outside her room. Their briefing is succinct: "She's still on the balcony, we think she took pills." I go in alone and find her outside the sliding door, on the balcony; she looks much too calm. She's big—nearly six feet tall and fairly heavy set, dressed in Levis and tennis shoes. I recognize her from one of the classes, but she was quiet and we never spoke at length.

First I try to establish rapport; she first listens, then tries to convince me there is no problem. Then I try to engage her in conversation; she moves closer to the edge, and keeps staring at the drop to the ground below. I can't hear any sirens yet. Then I attempt to get her to define the problem that she can't live with; she leans farther over the edge. Then I put my hand on her shoulder; she starts to cry. She lets me lead her back into her room.

She sits on a pillow on the floor, and cries a bit more. I realized there is an open bottle of pills on the coffee table. I ask her about them, and she suddenly lurches up and runs hard back toward the sliding door to the balcony. I tackle her before she gets there. I pin her down and she starts to relax, then to cry. I can finally hear a siren that sounds a long way off.

That's when she goes blank and stops breathing. After a moment of trying to wake her, I begin chest compressions. A minute later she takes in a huge gasp of air, and this time keeps breathing. Then she suddenly lurches up, throws me off, and heads for the sliding glass door a second time.

Again I tackle her and we crash down on the floor. She stops breathing, I do chest compressions, she surfaces and bolts. We repeat this death dance another three times—complete with arrested respiration—and my elbows and knees are skinned and swollen. Finally the paramedics and police enter, listen to my account and watch long enough to decide to transport her. She's loaded in the ambulance with an oxygen mask in place. I never see her again.

Frozen Falls

Robs, his friend Tony and I took off Friday and made the five-and-a-half-hour drive north on Hwy 395, up the east side of the Sierras. We listened to Andean flute music and watched the sun set over Mt. Whitney at about 5 pm, it being February. Then stopped for dinner at a gas station refrigerator case at about 7 p.m. in Bishop, saw the moon light up Mt. Tom before the Mammoth turn off around 8, and arrived at the camp site in Lee Vining at nearly 11. The tent was pitched on snow, and we squeezed in and crashed.

I'd learned the rudiments on Mt. Rainer the previous summer, but this was my chance to learn more technical ice climbing from two excellent climbers before my trip to climb the Aiguilles near Chamonix in August. I was, quite literally, placing myself in their hands. After an early breakfast at the climber's cafe, we hit the frozen falls.

The steep-sloped mountain raised some 500 feet above the trail. With Robs belaying from above on the nearly vertical second pitch, I found myself unable to go farther. My hands and forearms were so cramped, I couldn't hold my ice hammer tight enough for it to stick, and it spun loosely in my hands. My fingers had been slammed into the wall of ice so many times they bled into my climbing gloves and smeared the ice. I was desperately clinging on.

Tony reached me, and we clung together for a while as I tried to relax my shaking. "I don't know if I can make it," I grunted.

"You know," he said, "I never told you this, but I've always been jealous that I never went to Vietnam like you did." I looked over at him as if he were deranged. "Yeah, my older brother did, but I didn't," he continued. "I missed it. Jealous. Thought you should know."

I saw red. "You crazy fuck!"

I had to get away from him. I swung the ice hammer once more and somehow it stuck. I repositioned, pulled up, and kept on.

Redemption

Faith

On Good Friday we drew back from the firing line within feet of the shore, and put farther out into the Gulf of Tonkin. We refueled in the morning instead of after shelling at midnight— the rumor was a chaplain was being brought aboard to conduct services. I watched as he was dragged by bosun chair between the supply ship and our deck through more than one of the chaotic swells that funneled down the length of the gap. I wondered if this guy would listen to me.

I'd come to question my participation in the war, our boarding and sinking small coastal fishing and cargo boats, our nightly firing on fishing villages and free fire zones where it didn't matter who you hit. On the last time in port I'd met a group of medics from the resistance in the hospital who assured me they could get me out, get me home. I'd put them off for one more deployment, while I thought about it. Maybe I could speak with this man of god, get a clearer perspective.

In the service on the mess deck, he asked god to provide us courage and determination to continue our fight with the godless forces of oppression, and we sang old hymns of reassurance, "A Mighty Fortress Is Our God," and "How Great Thou Art." After the service I managed a chance to speak with him alone for a minute.

I told him of my conflict, my questioning, my concerns. I asked him whether a Christian should persist in this killing. "Son," he replied, "just who the hell are you to think you know more than your president, your generals and admirals?" He warmed to his task. "Just who the hell are you to question god in this matter?" He squeezed by me in the passageway and left.

Later I ran into my friend who knew I'd talked to the chaplain. He looked at me and grinned. "So," he shrugged. "how's your faith?"

Bill

After 9/11, I increasingly had to paint. A trauma consultant in the middle of the maelstrom of New York, I'd been stretched professionally, emotionally, spiritually. While I'd done much, I needed something to help me rebuild inside. I was carrying a place of great emptiness, a ruinous hole left by more than the collapse of buildings and lost lives. I'd seen too much unfold of who we really are as a people.

I'd taught art for years, but that had taken a back seat as the clinical work increased. Now it was time to get into it again, but this time seriously. I attended lectures and classes and demonstrations, hung out in museums, and worked alongside other artists. I exhibited my work in galleries, and even ran a gallery in a nearby city. But something in my work was still missing.

One day I wandered into the studio/gallery of Fr. Bill Moore. His work was stunning. A priest, a ministry of painting. Caught up in his work, I soon found myself talking. The next day I returned and showed him something I had done. I expected critique but he just stared and studied. Then he picked up a piece of matte board with a small square cut out of the center. Bill told me to hold it up close to my painting and move it around. To look for the small parts, and find bits in it, passages, that I truly loved.

I would watch him greet visitors to his studio, and Bill would join them in looking at his work. They would seek explanations, answers from him, but he was always more interested in what they had to say. He sought collaboration—the questions they both raised as he gently taught them to search the paintings, looking up close, running their hands over the surface, feeling with their hearts.

"Yes, It Is Ugly"

Maria Escobar, sculptor of the public statue of Father Damien—missionary to the leper colony on Moloka'i—called her own modernist work ugly, agreeing with dissenters on the commission to adopt a public tribute to the priest. They would have preferred a more "realistic, lifelike" work, a likeness of the handsome young Belgian priest when he had just arrived. They wanted a symbol of the spirit of Hawaii to stand before the State Capitol building. Hers was abrupt, with boxlike rigidity, the face scarred by the disease that soon killed him.

What drove the man to give all of himself? Was it the way the government had swept up anyone who showed the slightest symptoms, and banished them to the colony for life? Was it the capriciousness of life itself? How do you make retribution, amends for transgression, on your road to redemption? Do you go to cathedrals and sit in anonymous boxes and and chant the right homilies? Or do you face the inequities and chance cruelties of our lives and cultures squarely and devote yourself to serving the innocent with every thing you've got?

Redemption was never far from the mind of artist Fr. Bill Moore, from whose order Damien had come. Bill would walk the streets and railroad tracks of Pomona, keeping his eyes wide open for bits of cast-off material—worn metal parts, rusty screws and nails, broken sticks, buttons, torn cloth—and later incorporate them into sublime paintings of which the "worthless" were included and played an integral part. Later, he would invite the visitors to his studio to run their hands over the surface, to see deeply, feel the colors and open their hearts.

Ending the War

I'd decided that I wasn't ready yet to walk away. The war was immoral and a political cluster, the political resistance in port was ready to help me go home, but I couldn't let go. I'd decided to see it through. Changed rating to Boatswain's Mate striker, tried to become one of them. Hey diddle, diddle, right up the middle.

Repairs in port, taking on ammunition, painting, fixing, all the while the top officers get briefed on our next assignment. The bosun's mate in charge of my work area calls me and the sailors new to the ship to paint a section of the Port side quite high off the water. "Rig the scaffold, set 'em up with paint and rollers, and send the newbies over the side," he tells me. We climb up to the top, tie up the ropes, and lower the scaffold. Then I tie safety lines around the waists of the new guys, set them with rollers and buckets, and order them over.

One of the new kids is scared. He balks at climbing over the rail. It's a long way down. "I . . . I'm afraid of heights," he mumbles, and I notice he's pale. Shaking.

The petty officer on the deck below us has shifted from yelling to screaming at me, "I told you to get that son of a bitch over the side!"

I tell the kid again, but now he's crying and shaking all over. I'm questioning whether he actually would be safe out there. "Now! Get him over the side now, or I'll kick your ass in the paint locker!" the petty officer shrieks again, other sailors watching us.

And that's when I finally made up my mind. I roped up, took his roller and bucket, and went over the side despite the threats.

And after I was finished, I walked away.

In Paradisum

The sister walked us through the barrio to meet one of the parish nurses. Tall mango and banana trees and a thousand flowers lined the muddy dirt road. Their perfumes offset the mixed smells of charcoal brassieres and outhouses. Nipa huts stood on stilts to avoid being washed away during rainy season. A few pigs and chickens ran loose, as did several dogs.

Everyone loved the sister from the convent attached to the parish church, and many came out to greet her. We were introduced as visitors. One farmer climbed a palm to cut coconut to serve us. Another proudly displayed her new, indoor plumbing. An unattached commode without tank or seat sat on the bamboo see-through floor of the small room far too low for me to stand in and too narrow for me to sit on because the wall blocked my knees. An awkward backwards crouch allowed me to straddle the commode as if I were riding a horse. Flushing was accomplished by dipping a red Folger's coffee can into the adjacent 30-gallon oil drum, and pouring it into the toilet bowl. It worked fairly smoothly, forcing the contents to drop through the floor into a separate oil drum on the open ground below. The entire community nodded in approval.

The tour ended at the hut of the nurse. As we walked up, the sister explained how the woman's husband was driven away by the village because he was an angry drunk and would beat her. She raised four children in the one room hut, barely surviving by her part-time work at the parish clinic. Now the roof had fallen in when last month's storm came through, and the family was forced to sleep under a plastic tarp. They were all getting sick.

The woman came to the door. She seemed uncomfortable asking us in, and behind her we could see the plastic covering most of the floor with several small faces peering out. Someone coughed, another cried. The large hole in the roof let in the sky, and I could smell the mildew. The sister sensed the nurse's embarrassment and after a few questions about their health, and promises of food, we took our leave.

As we walked back past the trees and flowers, I inquired about repairs.

"I have a parishioner who has volunteered to fix the roof," she replied, "but we cannot raise the money for the thatch."

"How much would the materials cost?" I wondered.

"Twenty dollars, American."

I stopped and peeled the twenty off my roll.

Return

Elegy in White

Out of a pile of broken cinder blocks emerges a hand, perhaps digging out. I asked Larry, the artist, "What prompted that assemblage?" He fixed me with a gaze that went back years.

"I'd gone to a conference in D.C.," he said. "As we were gathering in front of the center to go in, you know, to register and get coffee, I heard the huge explosion. We looked across the Potomac at the Pentagon, with the huge hole in the side and smoke and people pouring out and taking cover, some under the freeway overpass." He looked down at his art piece. "It was ten years ago and I can't get rid of it. So I made this piece."

I looked at the piece and remembered my friend Victoria, a former flight nurse who'd been driving by and pulled in to see if she could help. She'd helped set up an aid station under that same overpass and ended up staying there all day. There were a few trees standing between them and the heat, and sights, and sounds. Precious little shade in the early September glare. I remembered working New York, not long after.

Healing

Tall, fragrant redwood trees growing close to the Gualala River reach toward sky; a place of the earth, spirit. Perhaps even magic. Some of us brought the burden of war, some abandonment, some the strain of living.

On the first day of the men's conference in the Redwoods, I'd arrived with a debilitating back spasm. An old injury had been exacerbated by long hours in airplane and car, and I was left unable to focus, to take part in activities, or even breathe. Fellow conference attendees attempted to help. Chris, my Episcopal priest/therapist/truck driver friend tried prayer, my friend Martin, osteopath by trade, tried adjustment.

By the second day I was desperate. Someone took me to see John. John was said to be a shaman; he said healer. John listened to my story, agreed to try to help, then led me down to the river that snaked through the conference ground. We walked around a bit until John found a suitable place, a column in the embankment where the flooding river had eddied, and cut a cylindrical space confined on most sides ten feet high, creating an echo chamber I could stand in. I did.

"Here's what I'm going to do," he told me. "I'm going to experiment with tonal and pitch variations until I find which frequencies you respond to. Then I'm going to shout at you in those frequencies. I don't know what you'll experience," he said, "but you'll probably know when we are there. I will too. Then we'll focus on that."

He did. I stood still in the embankment cylinder, and he began to shout at me. He went higher and lower until I started to see a band of vertical light which was yellowish in color and had a broader area which traveled up and down according to John's pitch. His voice was loud and harsh. When he got to a certain point the light, and my entire body, trembled. John knew that and told me to brace myself. He then kept at that precise pitch, louder and louder. The sound of the river, the wind, the images in my mind, all swirled together until it all reached a peak. The light column shook and began to explode. I almost fell down with the intensity. Then silence, peace.

It was gone.

Michaelson's Legs

Glass sculptures, from several inches to a foot tall, stopped me in my tracks. Their color and shape drew me past the normal range of artwork at the monthly gallery crawl in Pomona. Two pieces set at a little beyond right angles, fused at one end. A third piece vertical. Where the vertical piece intersected the other two, they were not fused, but rather bound together with rough cloth, dirty, sometimes with leather thong. Then I realized, they were bones.

They each were somewhat different, yet each basically the same pattern. Variously colored, variously configured, the pieces spoke an unspoken story. The artist, Michaelson, was available, but wasn't much for small talk. Tall, quiet, nice enough, he spoke about the materials and techniques he used in making the pieces, where they'd shown, how they'd been received. Then he'd move on to the next visitor.

Later I was able to speak with him and found out his story. After several halting return visits Michaelson finally told me how he had served in the Army during the Vietnam war. A forward observer, he'd slipped and fallen down a mountainside twisting in vines and breaking his knee. Alone, he'd had to bind his protruding broken bones with "field expedient materials"—read that dirty cloth, vine, and leather thong. He'd worked his way back to his unit—days of stumbling and crawling with great effort and pain, avoiding capture, eating and drinking what he could find, rebinding his leg, again and again. He learned more than he ever wanted about fragility and the delicate balance of our material existence.

For ten years after his release from hospitals and therapies, this man could not speak of his experience. Finally he found aesthetic expression and a medium, glass, that allowed him to begin to tell others. He would lose himself in his work, pulling molten glass bones for hours and days.

Going on after Jackson

"Don't ever schedule me to follow Jackson onstage," I told Pete. I had just given what felt to me to be my worst class ever, at the disaster training foundation in Maryland. The lecture seemed pedantic, my examples and illustrations boring, my jokes had fallen flat—the applause polite, at best. I knew it wasn't just me. I had walked up to the microphone after Jackson.

The man had been amazing. He turned his section of the course "Legal Liabilities of Disaster Workers" into a side show. He was animated, his slides were high-impact cartoons, and they were really funny. He was the Robin Williams of lawyering—rapid fire. He'd mentioned his asshole supervisor, and held up a picture of a naked someone bending over, displaying their aforementioned body cavity. He had the audience rolling. All the right content got covered and when he concluded, handing out the speaker evaluation slips, he held up a large photo of his little girl, and reminded them he was hoping to send her to college.

"You've got to see it from my perspective." Peter Smalley, the foundation's course coordinator took another sip of his microbrewery ale and shook his head. "I can't get anyone to follow him. I rotate everybody through. This was just your turn." Another sip. "Let me give you the back story."

And he did. It turns out Jackson is actually a motorcycle cop, working shifts in a nearby city. He's always loved being on a bike, and despite his success as a part time lawyer, wouldn't quit his day patrol job. High stimulus need, loves the excitement.

Jackson wasn't always so outgoing. Initially quiet, inhibited and retiring, the guy would avoid talking to people whenever he could. One day, on a high speed pursuit, he entered an intersection and tangled with a sports car that ran the light and plowed into him. Thrown from his bike, Jackson slid into a curb head first. Massive head trauma. Should have died on the spot.

Yet here he is, a changed man. Although the neurologists can't explain it, Jackson's neurons re-knit, and his colleagues say perhaps better than before. Somehow he recovered to be able to ride again. He eventually got his job back. And then he began law school part time. And completed it. Jackson now represents fellow officers in court, when he's not fighting crime from the back of his motorcycle. Recovered and then some, the formerly shy and retiring one now bounds on stage ready to dazzle us all.

Spectre

It was a simple divorce. No kids, no property to speak of, no fat investment funds to split. Purpose and fervor had gone, replaced by a flat regret; the relationship was now simply over. They were from different tribes, backgrounds, cultures—different futures. Now was the time to get out.

He'd spent the night in a motel in Indio with a small caliber pistol, seeking the warm evening breeze he once knew there. They'd stayed among the tall palms, dancing to the sound of dry fronds in the gusts. Instead it remained too hot long into the night and the Santa Ana winds blew hard. He'd spent it drinking in his room, watching TV and finally sleeping. Now it was getting light and he'd driven to a beach along the Salton Sea that his parents had taken him to several lifetimes ago.

It had changed, though, like everything else. Even in the violet pink light of dawn, the inland sea was lined with dead fish. The offshore Santa Ana winds blew the waves flat and the gulls were nearly silent. As the sun started up, he could make out a few people wandering, looking for things, evidently without direction.

He thought of the desert art installation he'd driven by yesterday. A reddish-orange metal cuboid, perhaps the size of a shipping container, perched in a wash and detached from it's surroundings. The creosote, the rows of giant wind turbines, the distant peaks, were all almost reflected on the shiny surface. It was empty, the surface being the message. A giant erasure.

As foam and washed up detritus began to glow with sunrise, he wondered what that huge chrome/red cube would look like out there, rising from the water.

EPILOGUE

I am old enough now to taste the brevity of history. I have lived the majority of my life in the town in which I grew up. I have lived through well over half the life of my town, and nearly half the life of my state. World War II was not yet finished when I began, and the Berlin Airlift had yet to begin. In my eighteenth year I sat on a remnant of the Remagen Bridge that my father had crossed during the week in which I was born, not long before. I watched the news when Sputnik was launched and when Kennedy was shot. I read about Jackson Pollock and read Jack Kerouac.

My ancestors lived the battlefields in Europe, and the Civil War and Revolutionary War here. My father, the Battle of the Bulge. My generation, my cousins and I, stumbled into Vietnam. I kept up that stumbling as I worked on-scene on the large-scale disasters of the end of the 20th century and beginning of the 21st. We share a legacy of stain. I have spoken with some of those ancestors in the Eucalyptus grove north of town, where I retreat to try and find sense.

I perch on the far western edge of my continent, washed up by successive waves of migration. Before this we lived on Midwest plains, in Kentucky and Quebec, New York and Jamestown. Before that, Scotland, Ireland and England. And before that, Denmark and France, and maybe the deep forests of Germany, before it was called Germany. And before that, who knows? Celts, Picts, when the last ice finally left? My grandparents and parents reached the trail's dead end in Hollywood, Disneyland, and the Santa Monica Pier. Now what? If we were to sail west and over the bigger pond, past the dateline, the lands of China, the Middle East, and back to Western Europe again, that foggy place from which we began would be as indistinguishable as Catalina Island in a driving rain.

Appreciation

This book would not have been possible without the assistance of Mark Givens and Dennis Callaci of Bamboo Dart Press, the collaborative efforts of John Brantingham and Kate Flannery, the encouragement of BDP's other authors, and the support of Susan Ilsley. Thank you all.

About the Author

Kendall Johnson, former firefighter with military experience, served as traumatic stress consultant—often in the field—specializing in Incident Command System Class I & II commands. Initially working with individual and small team line per-sonnel, His responsibilities evolved to provide consultation to field commanders and their operational teams, and, when necessary, provide intervention in order to maintain team effectiveness in the midst of incidents that had turned traumatic. He has lectured in fire houses, hospitals, emergency service institutes, conferences, government training facilities, universities, here and abroad.

He trained others in the principles he developed. Dr. Johnson was Adjunct Faculty member at the California State Training Institute (Governor's Office of Emergency Services), served on the Faculty of the International Critical Incident Stress Foundation, and was Associate Professor in the Master's Degree program in Emergency Services Management at California State University, Long Beach.

He has authored a number of professional papers, seven books in the treatment of traumatic stress, school crisis management, and recovery. Recently Dr. Johnson retired from teaching to pursue painting, photography, and writing. In that capacity he has written five literary books of artwork and poetry, and one in art history.

BAMBOO DART PRESS

112 N. Harvard Ave. #65
Claremont, CA 91711

chapbooks@bamboodartpress.com
www.bamboodartpress.com

www.ingramcontent.com/pod-product-compliance
Lightning Source LLC
Chambersburg PA
CBHW081241020426
42331CB00013B/3248